Classy Clip Art

Illustrations by Dale Bargmann and Robert M. Moyer

Loveland, Colorado

Classy Clip Art

Credits
Edited by Eugene C. Roehlkepartain
Cover and interior designed by Jill Christopher

Library of Congress Cataloging-in-Publication Data
Bargmann, Dale, 1947-
Classy clip art / illustrations by Dale Bargmann and Robert M. Moyer.
    p.
    Includes index.
    ISBN 1-55945-020-7
    1. Church bulletins. 2. Church newsletters—Publishing. 3. Copy art. I. Moyer,
    Robert M., 1924-   II. Title.
Bv653.3.B37   1991
254.3—dc20   91-14206
                                                                    CIP

Printed in the United States of America

Contents

Introduction

Imagine the scene when people receive their mail. They rummage through a whole stack of slick-looking magazines, "junk" mail with splashy art and headlines, and personal mail. And ... oh ... the youth group or church newsletter.

Will they pick it up? Can it really catch their attention in the midst of all the other material they receive?

With clip art from *Classy Clip Art* adding interest and a professional touch, the newsletter (or poster or flier or bulletin insert or handout) will get the attention it deserves. And you don't need art and design expertise to use it. Just follow these simple steps:

1. Write the information you want to convey. Keep it short and to the point. Include all important information for events and classes, including ...
- time;
- date; and
- place.

2. Select art for the item you want to illustrate. The index on page 121 will guide you to the specific topics illustrated in this book. The art is divided into the following categories:

● *Church Life*—Art for Sunday school, youth group, Bible study, worship, choir and other regular events in church life.

● *Special Events*—Art for special events, including talent shows, retreats, ski trips, sports, concerts and much more.

● *Hot Topics*—Art on youth-meeting topics, such as peer pressure, drugs, dating, love, family and more.

● *Service, Outreach and Missions*—Art for service ministries, including soup kitchens and visiting the elderly, people with disabilities and others.

● *Holidays, Seasons and Celebrations*—Art for everything from New Year's to Christmas to graduation.

● *Newsletters and Notes*—Dozens of tidbits to brighten up newsletters, including ready-to-use newsletter designs, greetings and more.

3. Type the information (or generate it on your computer) in the form you want, leaving room for the artwork. Think about creative ways to "wrap" the type around the art. Carefully read what you typed for clarity, accuracy and typographical errors.

4. Clip the right-size art. If you have a photocopier with enlargement and reduction capabilities, use it to make the art the exact size you need.

5. Glue the art into place. Using rubber cement will allow you to adjust the art without tearing it.

6. Duplicate and distribute the information. Then wait for people to notice the professional work!

Church Life

YOU'RE THE MISSING INGREDIENT

lend a hand

WE NEED YOU

lend a hand

WE NEED YOU

WE'RE LOOKING FOR A FEW GOOD VOLUNTEERS

lend a hand

WE'RE LOOKING FOR A FEW GOOD VOLUNTEERS

YOU'RE THE MISSING INGREDIENT

YOU'RE THE MISSING INGREDIENT

WE NEED YOU

WE'RE LOOKING FOR A FEW GOOD VOLUNTEERS

BE A
CLOWN

Puppet Power

Puppet Power

BE A
CLOWN

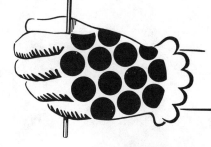

Puppet Power

BE A
CLOWN

Make a Noticeable Difference– Join the Choir

TAKE NOTE

TAKE NOTE

Make a Noticeable Difference– Join the Choir

Make a Noticeable Difference– Join the Choir

TAKE NOTE

VaCAtion
BiBle SCHOOL

VaCAtion
BiBle SCHOOL

VaCAtioN
BiBle SCHOOL

Your Most Important Conversation

Pray Together

Your Most Important Conversation

Pray Together

Pray Together

Your Most Important Conversation

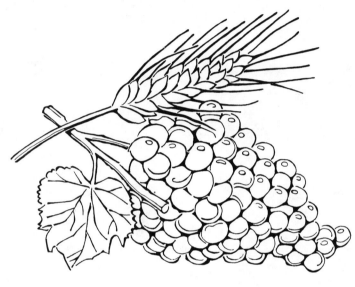

CELEBRATE!

IN TIMES OF NEED

IN TIMES OF NEED

WITH OUR PRAYERS

CELEBRATE!

IN TIMES OF NEED

CELEBRATE!

WITH OUR PRAYERS

WITH OUR PRAYERS

REACH OUT IN FELLOWSHIP

REACH OUT IN FELLOWSHIP

FATHER SON SPIRIT

ALLELUIA

FATHER SON SPIRIT

ALLELUIA

FATHER SON SPIRIT

ALLELUIA

REACH OUT IN FELLOWSHIP

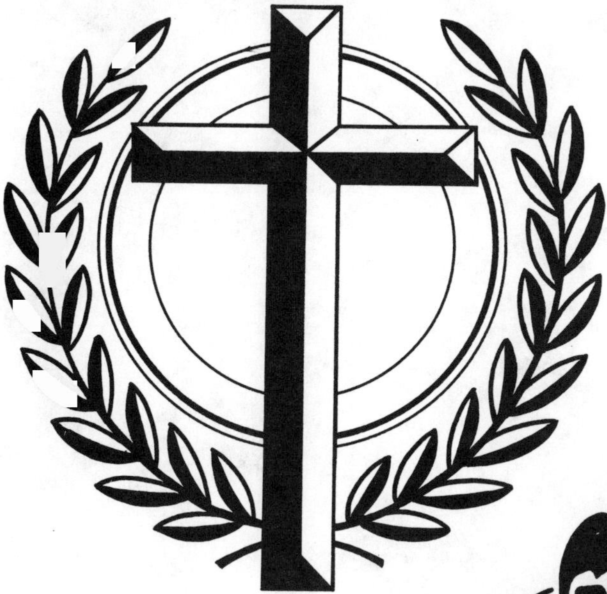
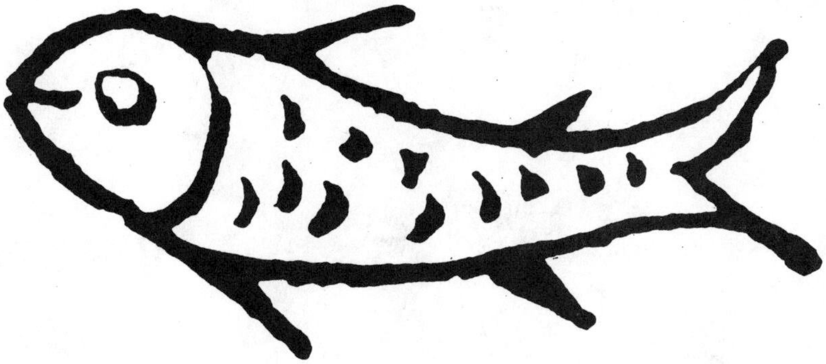
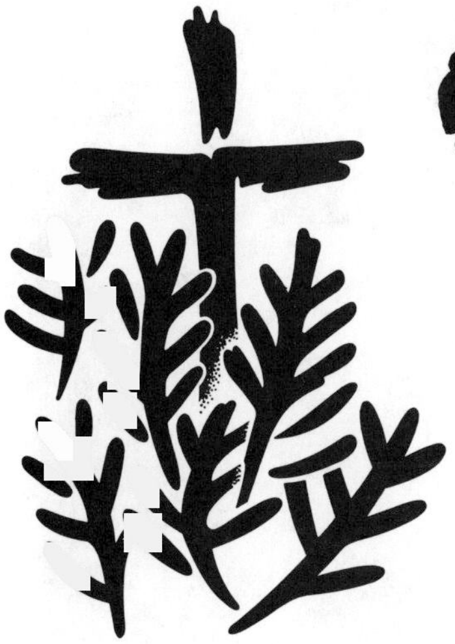
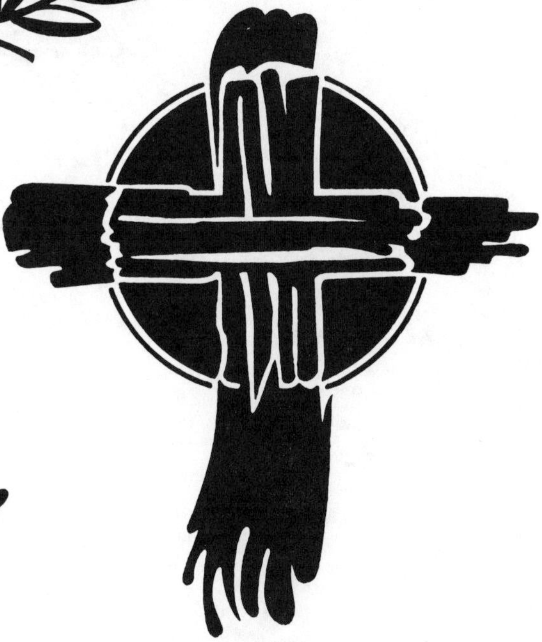
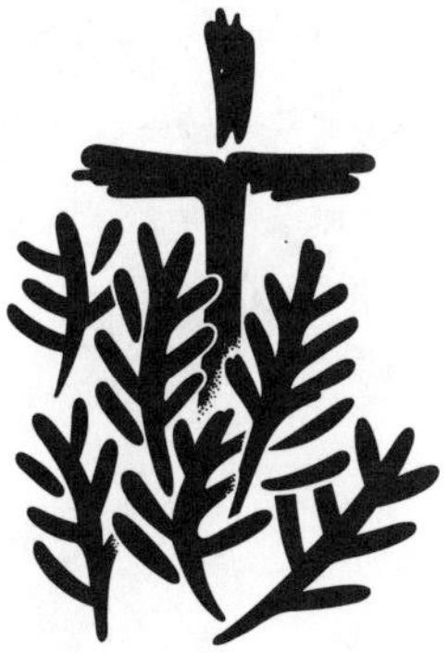
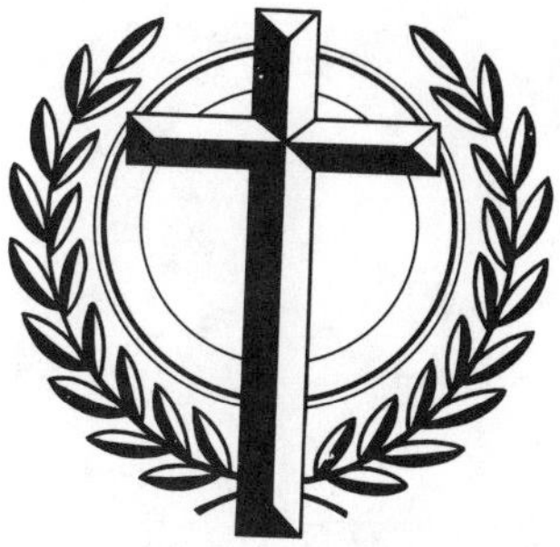
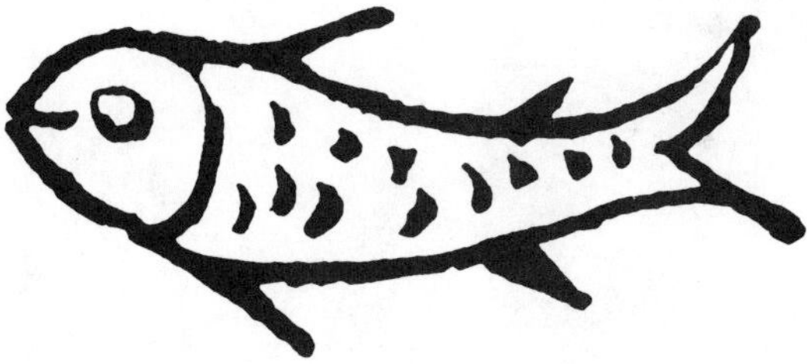
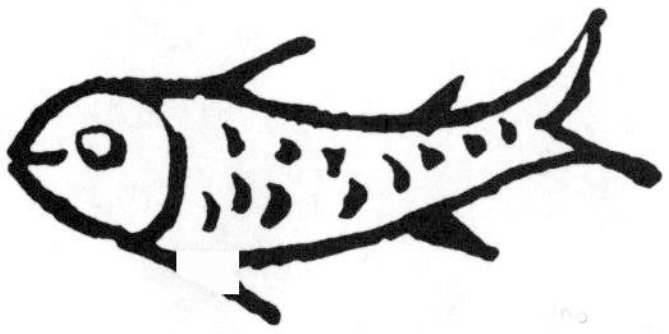
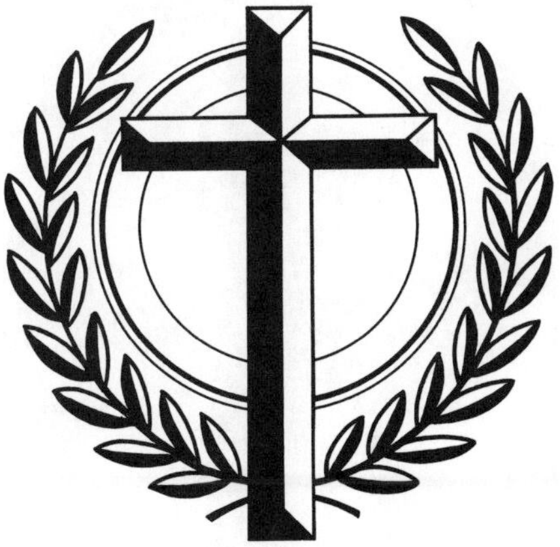
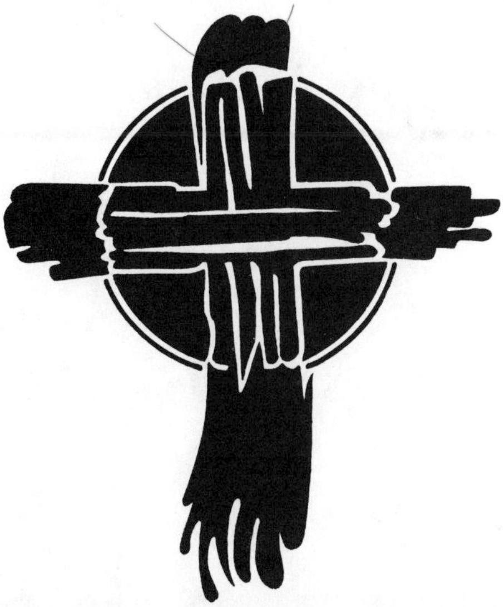
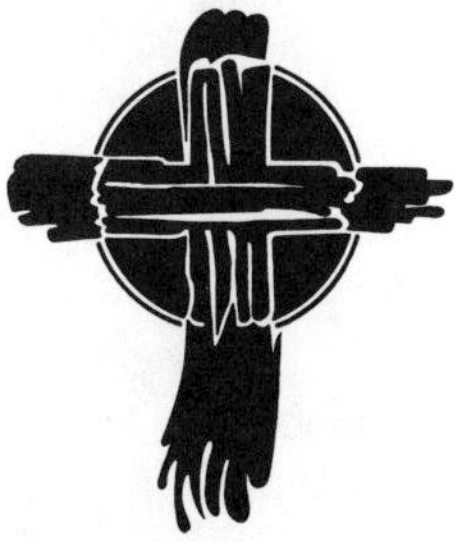
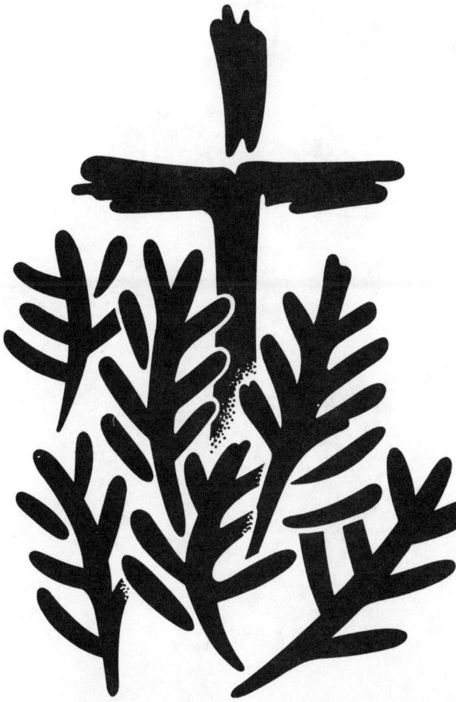

Special Events

NOW SHOWING

LOOK WHO'S COMING

WE'RE SEARCHING FOR STARS

LOOK WHO'S COMING

NOW SHOWING

WE'RE SEARCHING FOR STARS

WE'RE SEARCHING FOR STARS

LOOK WHO'S COMING

NOW SHOWING

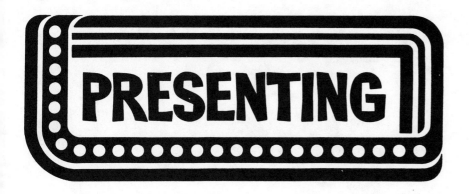

SKI SPREE

SNOOSH

SURF'S UP!

SNOOSH

SKI SPREE

SNOOSH

SURF'S UP!

SKI SPREE

SURF'S UP!

GOING PLACES

We're | Going | Places

We're | Going | Places

GOING PLACES

GOING PLACES

We're | Going | Places

Beat the **HEAT**

Eat this
Up

Eat this
Up

Beat the **HEAT**

EAT
OUT

EAT
OUT

Eat this
Up

Beat the **HEAT**

EAT
OUT

Raft-OAR Else

Raft-OAR Else

Raft-OAR Else

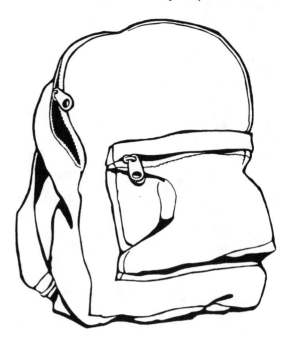

Family Fun Fest

Hit the road

Family Fun Fest

Hit the road

BIKE BONANZA

BIKE BONANZA

Hit the road

BIKE BONANZA

STRIKE!

JOIN THE TEAM

STRIKE!

WE'RE HAVING A BALL

WE'RE HAVING A BALL

JOIN THE TEAM

STRIKE!

JOIN THE TEAM

WE'RE HAVING

A BALL

We're Having a Ball

We're Having a Ball

We're Having a Ball

We're Having a BALL!

We're Having a BALL!

We're Having a BALL!

Make Points With Us

Make Points With Us

Make Points With Us

We're Having a BALL!

We're Having a BALL!

We're Having a BALL!

Make Points With Us

Make Points With Us

Make Points With Us

Hot Topics

Hot Topics

I've Always Wondered

I've Always Wondered

WHAT ARE FRIENDS FOR?

Do you fit in?

Lean on Me

WHAT ARE FRIENDS FOR?

WHAT ARE FRIENDS FOR?

Do you fit in?

Lean on Me

Lean on Me

Do you fit in?

GETTING ALONG WITH PARENTS

GETTING ALONG WITH PARENTS

GETTING ALONG WITH PARENTS

All in the Family

All in the Family

GETTING ALONG WITH PARENTS

GETTING ALONG WITH PARENTS

GETTING ALONG WITH PARENTS

All in the Family

WHEN YOUR PARENTS DIVORCE

PULLED IN TWO

WHEN YOUR PARENTS DIVORCE

Oh brother, Oh sister

Oh brother, Oh sister

WHEN YOUR PARENTS DIVORCE

PULLED IN TWO

Oh brother, Oh sister

PULLED IN TWO

What Do You Hear?

Drum Up Enthusiasm

What Do You Hear?

Drum Up Enthusiasm

Drum Up Enthusiasm

What Do You Hear?

ARE YOU
BOOKED
TONIGHT?

School
Daze

grAD+e
expectations
AB-

grAD+e
expectations
AB-

ARE YOU
BOOKED
TONIGHT?

School
Daze

ARE YOU
BOOKED
TONIGHT?

grAD+e
expectations
AB-

School
Daze

STRESSED OUT

STRESSED OUT

STRESSED OUT

UP IN SMOKE

Drinking & Driving

IT'S NOT A GAME

Drinking & Driving

IT'S NOT A GAME

UP IN SMOKE

UP IN SMOKE

THE DEADLY BOTTLE

THE DEADLY BOTTLE

Drinking & Driving

IT'S NOT A GAME

THE DEADLY BOTTLE

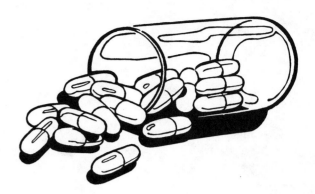

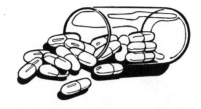

AIDS:
A SCARY
KILLER

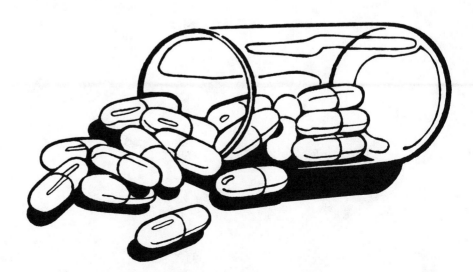

AIDS:
A SCARY
KILLER

AIDS:
A SCARY
KILLER

AIDS:
A SCARY
KILLER

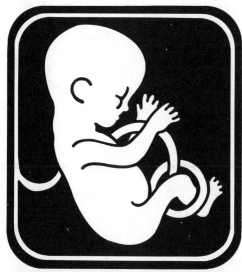

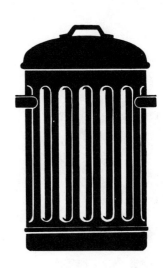

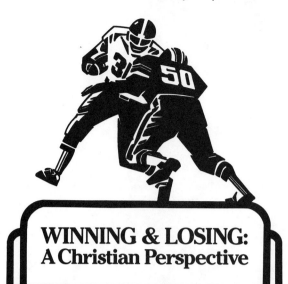

WINNING & LOSING:
A Christian Perspective

WINNING & LOSING:
A Christian Perspective

TEMPLE MAINTENANCE

TEMPLE MAINTENANCE

TEMPLE MAINTENANCE

WINNING & LOSING:
A Christian Perspective

ANOREXIA:
Too Thin to Eat

FACED WITH A FIGHT

WORK: DOES I+ MAKE ¢ENT$?

WORK: DOES I+ MAKE ¢ENT$?

FACED WITH A FIGHT

WORK: DOES I+ MAKE ¢ENT$?

FACED WITH A FIGHT

ANOREXIA:
Too Thin to Eat

ANOREXIA:
Too Thin to Eat

Service, Outreach and Missions

Need a friend?

Need a friend?

Need a friend?

SAY THANKS WITH GIVING

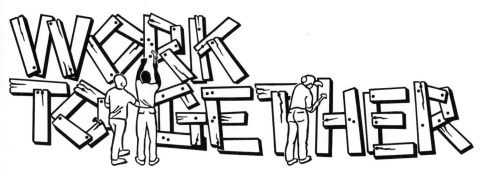

SAY THANKS WITH GIVING

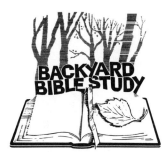

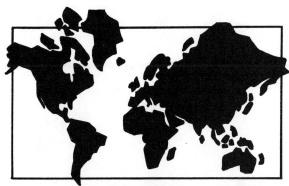

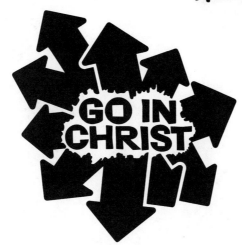

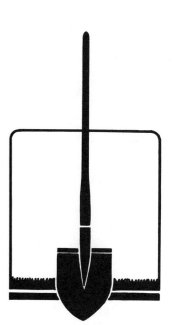

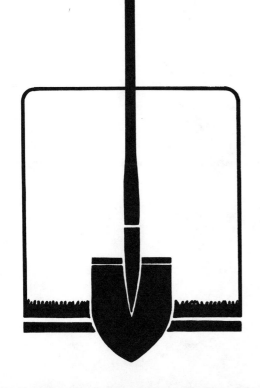

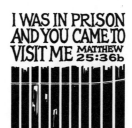

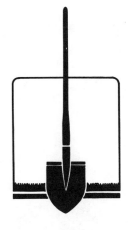

YOU CAN MAKE A DIFFERENCE!

YOU CAN MAKE A DIFFERENCE!

Serving Christ by Serving Others

Serving Christ by Serving Others

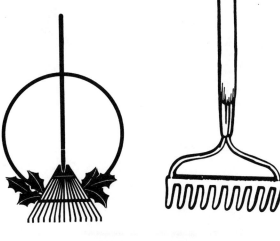

Serving Christ by Serving Others

YOU CAN MAKE A DIFFERENCE!

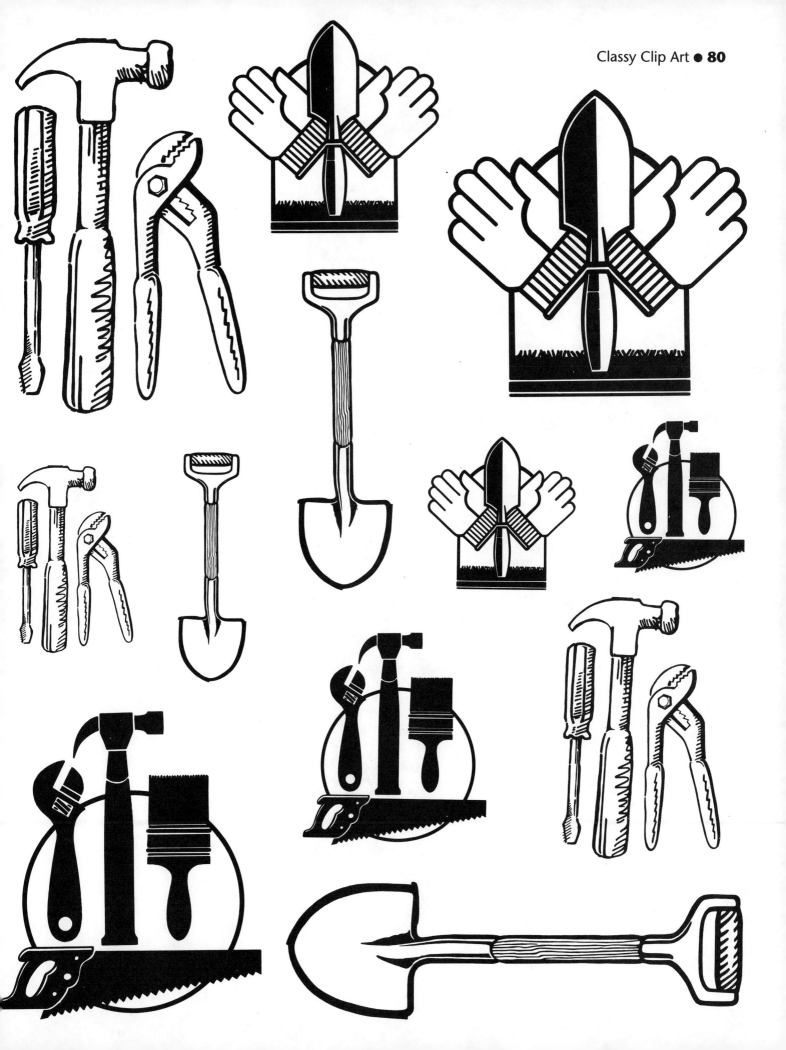

Holidays, Seasons and Celebrations

He Had A Dream... Do You?

Celebrate the New Year

HE HAD A DREAM... DO YOU?

Celebrate the New Year

HE HAD A DREAM... DO YOU?

ST. PATRICK'S DAY

ST. PATRICK'S DAY

COME, HOLY SPIRIT

COME, HOLY SPIRIT

COME, HOLY SPIRIT

ST. PATRICK'S DAY

Prepare THE WAY

Ash Wednesday

HOLY WEEK

Prepare THE WAY

Ash Wednesday

HOLY WEEK

HOLY WEEK

Ash Wednesday

Prepare THE WAY

Maundy Thursday

Maundy Thursday

Maundy Thursday

Independence DAY

Independence **Day**

Independence Day

Independence DAY

Independence DAY

BACK TO SCHOOL

BACK TO SCHOOL

BACK TO SCHOOL

Waiting for the Savior

Waiting for the Savior

The greatest gift

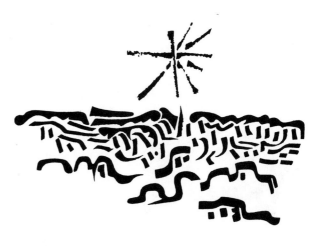

He is Born!

He is Born!

The greatest gift

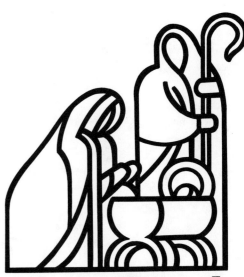

He is Born!

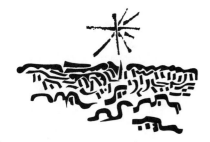

The greatest gift

The gift of Christmas

The gift of Christmas

Merry Christmas

The gift of Christmas

Merry Christmas

Merry Christmas

EPIPHANY

EPIPHANY

EPIPHANY

Newsletters and Notes

YOU'RE A STAR

A STELLAR PERFORMANCE!

YOU'RE A STAR

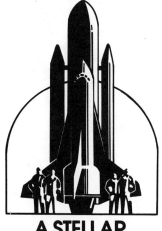

A STELLAR PERFORMANCE!

YOU'RE A STAR

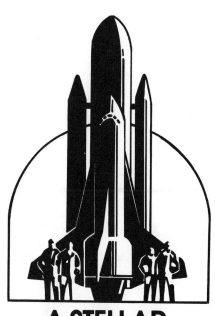

A STELLAR PERFORMANCE!

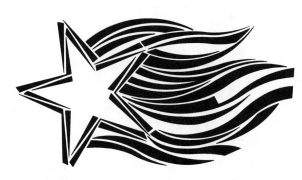

WEDDING BELLS

Engaged

WEDDING BELLS
ARE RINGING

JUST HiTcHED

JUST HiTcHED

JUST HiTcHED

WEDDING BELLS

Engaged

WEDDING BELLS

WEDDING BELLS
ARE RINGING

WEDDING BELLS
ARE RINGING

Engaged

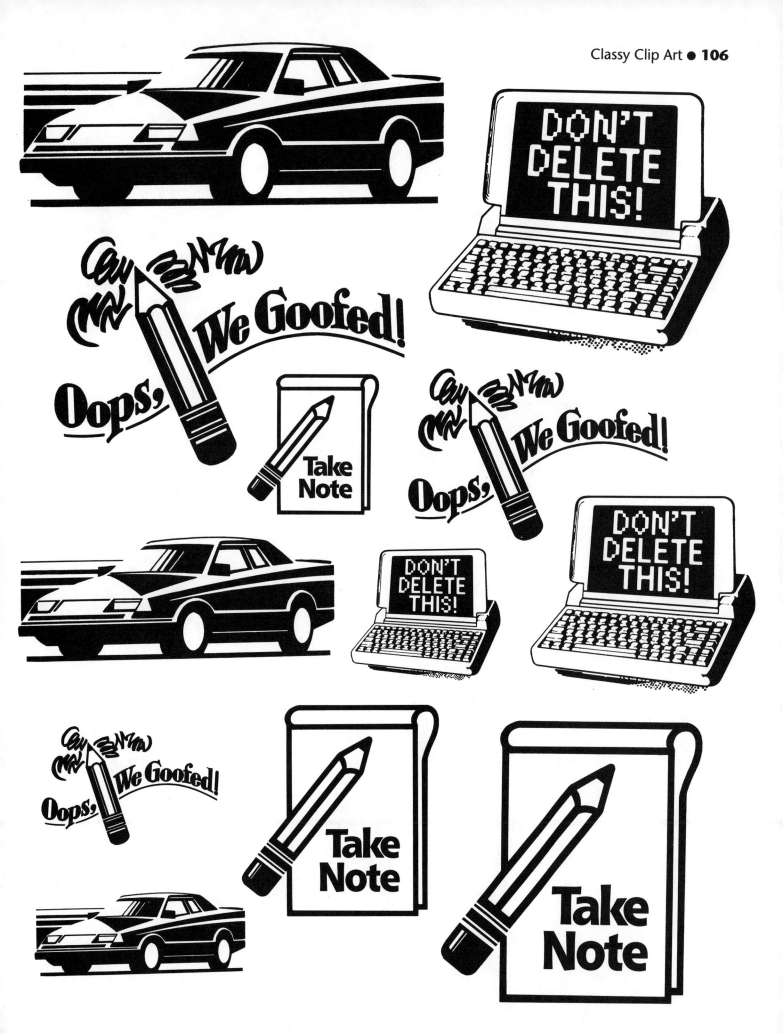

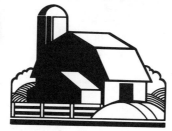

LOOKING AHEAD

IN CONCERT

LOOKING AHEAD

VELCOME

SYMPATHY

LOOKING AHEAD

New Members

SYMPATHY

New Members

MARK YOUR CALENDAR

New Members

SYMPATHY

MARK YOUR CALENDAR

YOUTH DIRECTORY

MARK YOUR CALENDAR

YOUTH DIRECTORY

YOUTH DIRECTORY

IN OUR PRAYERS

HOSPITALIZED

NEW MEMBERS

IN OUR PRAYERS

VISITORS

NEW MEMBERS

Guess what's Coming

VISITORS

Guess what's Coming

VISITORS

MARK YOUR CALENDAR✓

Guess what's Coming

OUR SYMPATHIES

MARK YOUR CALENDAR✓

OUR SYMPATHIES

JANUARY
FEBRUARY
MARCH
APRIL
MAY
JUNE
JULY
AUGUST
SEPTEMBER
OCTOBER
NOVEMBER
DECEMBER

SUNDAY
MONDAY
TUESDAY
WEDNESDAY
THURSDAY
FRIDAY
SATURDAY

SUNDAY
MONDAY
TUESDAY
WEDNESDAY
THURSDAY
FRIDAY
SATURDAY

SUNDAY MONDAY
TUESDAY WEDNESDAY
THURSDAY FRIDAY
SATURDAY

SUNDAY
MONDAY
TUESDAY
WEDNESDAY
THURSDAY
FRIDAY
SATURDAY

JANUARY	JULY
FEBRUARY	AUGUST
MARCH	SEPTEMBER
APRIL	OCTOBER
MAY	NOVEMBER
JUNE	DECEMBER

JANUARY
FEBRUARY
MARCH
APRIL
MAY
JUNE
JULY
AUGUST
SEPTEMBER
OCTOBER
NOVEMBER
DECEMBER

JANUARY
FEBRUARY
MARCH
APRIL
MAY
JUNE
JULY
AUGUST
SEPTEMBER
OCTOBER
NOVEMBER
DECEMBER

JANUARY	JULY
FEBRUARY	AUGUST
MARCH	SEPTEMBER
APRIL	OCTOBER
MAY	NOVEMBER
JUNE	DECEMBER

JANUARY	JULY
FEBRUARY	AUGUST
MARCH	SEPTEMBER
APRIL	OCTOBER
MAY	NOVEMBER
JUNE	DECEMBER

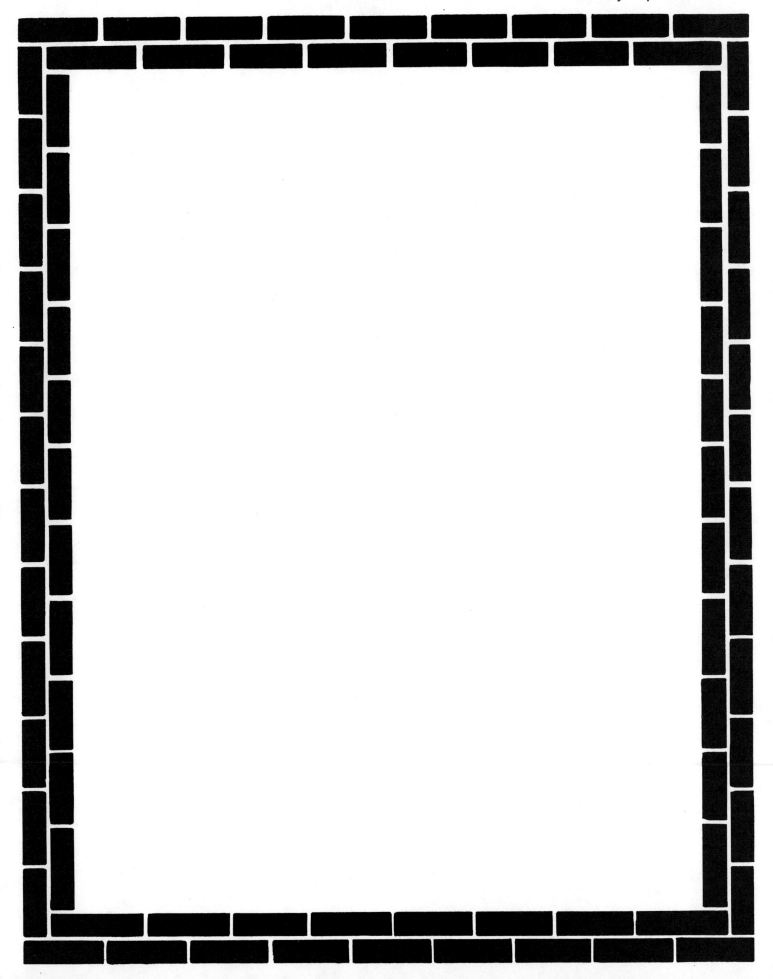

Index

Creative Resources from

OUTRAGEOUS CLIP ART FOR YOUTH MINISTRY

Rand Kruback

Get hundreds of kooky clip art cartoons that teeter on the brink of bizarre. Delight your kids with easy-to-create, off-the-wall newsletters and announcements.

Get loads of unusual program ideas from this crazy clip art, including . . .

- Burger bash
- Roller derby
- Lunch munch
- Pie party
- Water war
- Taco fiesta
- Bus brigade
- Frisbee fling
- Pancake feed

You'll grab kids' and parents' attention fast with not-so-typical ways to say,

Oops!
Be there!
Happy Birthday!
S-s-s-surprise!

Thanks a lot
Missed you
Come and get it!
Why me, Lord?

Add spark and spice to all your printed pieces. Boost attendance and excitement—with kid-pleasing art straight from the outer limits of Rand Kruback's bizarre imagination.

ISBN 0-931529-39-5 $14.95

YOUTH MINISTRY CLIP ART

Steve Hunt and Dave Adamson, The Church Art Works™

Give your printed pieces a bold new look—fast. You'll get hundreds of ready-to-use illustrations in all sizes. Headlines. Cartoons. Borders. Everything you need to jazz up your handouts. And it's as easy as 1-2-3.

1. Choose your clip art.
2. Cut it out.
3. Paste it on the page.

Then head to the nearest photocopier and produce professional-looking, attention-getting newsletters, posters, fliers, calendars, announcements and more.

ISBN 0-931529-26-3 $14.95

GROUP'S BUILD-A-MEETING BOOK, VOL. 1

from the Editors of Group Books

When you need a complete meeting ... a quick crowdbreaker ... or a monthly programming idea ... reach for **Group's Build-a-Meeting Book, Vol. 1**.

You'll choose from hundreds of proven programming ideas ... quick and easy-to-use activities ... exciting themes for special events ... and more.

Part 1 is chockful of creative ideas for custom-built meetings. Simply pick 'n' choose the program elements you need—and PRESTO—your programming's done. You'll choose from winning ...

- crowdbreakers and games
- affirmations
- closings
- and more
- discussion-starters
- prayers
- snack ideas

In Part 2 you'll find loads of fun programming ideas for each month of the year—from January to December. Use these special-events programs to cement relationships in your group. Grow kids' faith commitments. And draw young people closer to God.

Plus, you get a handy "Meeting Planner" and "Build-a-Meeting Log Sheet" to help you stay organized. Use **Group's Build-a-Meeting Book, Vol. 1** to help you construct winning programs for years to come.

ISBN 1-55945-052-5 $7.95

These and other Group products are available at your local Christian bookstore. Or order direct from the publisher. Write Group, Box 481, Loveland, CO 80539. Please add $3 for postage and handling per order. Colorado residents add 3% sales tax.